Echoes of Nature

Larry Ellington

AuthorHouse™
1663 Liberty Drive
Bloomington, IN 47403
www.authorhouse.com
Phone: 833-262-8899

Because of the dynamic nature of the Internet, any web addresses or links contained in this book may have changed
since publication and may no longer be valid. The views expressed in this work are solely those of the author and do
not necessarily reflect the views of the publisher, and the publisher hereby disclaims any responsibility for them.

Any people depicted in stock imagery provided by Getty Images are models,
and such images are being used for illustrative purposes only.
Certain stock imagery © Getty Images.

This book is printed on acid-free paper.

ISBN: 978-1-7283-7787-2 (sc)
ISBN: 978-1-7283-7785-8 (hc)
ISBN: 978-1-7283-7786-5 (e)

Library of Congress Control Number: 2023901222

Print information available on the last page.

Published by AuthorHouse 01/30/2023

authorHOUSE

Images on a Rainy Night

Western skies, vast in copious gray shades, ring with tympanic thunder.
Bolts, bright and jagged split the dark, moist, opulent air,
Illuminating the night scenes!
Desert pavements, glistening with wetness;
Windows distorted with beads of crystal rain!

Dogs cowering,
Shivering,
Shuddering

Huddled in trash can alleys, sniffling and sneezing.
Lights shimmering peacefully in mirrored sidewalk squares,
Virtually exploding in prismatic colors!

Damp odors permeate the air with a strange freshness,
As cool raindrops caress our senses!
When suddenly we realize.
There are no rainbows at night!

My Hesperus

No shedded tear
For me my dear
I've captained my own fate!
And for my crew
I chose just you
To help me pull the weight

But you're not strong
And can't last long
Without love and affection
You took the course
Of least remorse
To find a new direction

Now we're apart
In mind and heart
Our ship is rent asunder
My Hesperus
Came back to us
And sank amid our thunder

Now she was lost
And tempest tossed
She drowned beneath the sea
And so with us
My Hesperus
Is slowly drowning me!

So Glad to be Alive

The streamlet flowed though ferns and grass
Wending it's merry way
From thawed out ice and snow it formed
For it is Spring today!

And as in cycles of the past
Tomorrow will arrive
To be a Summer full of sun
So good to be alive!

The streams that flowed in early spring
Will dry up soon you'll see
Until next year when snow and ice
Will bring them back to thee!

Whats Best for You Instead

I sat with death one lonely night
And looked him in the eye.
He was a rather fearsome sight
Death came to watch me die!

He wanted me to join him on
A journey of great length?
When something in me wished him gone
It must have been a strength!

A strength of will, a strength of love
A strength not felt before
Perhaps the strength of God himself
Was needed for this chore?

So when death comes to greet you
Remember what I've said,
And look to God, for he will do
What's best for you instead!

Beyond Reality

I dwelt upon the pale clock face,
One cold Novembers eve
My mind fell gently to the ground
Like Autumns colored leaves

They skittered into windy swirls
And danced a Highland fling
The movement made an eerie sound
Like angels on the wing

They rustled through the dry brown grass
With a stealth not shone before
They found the secret crevices
Behind the padlocked door

They danced like ghosts of sheerest white
In images bizarre
At Places that do not exist
On this Ephemeral star

My nightmare ends abruptly
The ringing seems aloof
My gaze lands on that clock face
I need no further proof

If time controls our daily lives
Then dreams must set us free
To go beyond times limits
Beyond reality

I Saw a Bird

I saw a bird

A lonely bird

In Aprils winter tree!

The branches bare

Left him up there

For anyone to see!

I thought how cruel

That Scarlett jewel

To tease my eyes this way!

And pull my mind

Out from behind

My thoughts of yesterday!

Where Love Will Never Cease

I think about the good times
And those that come between!
The ups and downs of lovers
Like we have always been!

The ups are so delightful
With loves eternal bliss
The downs are so disheartening
Where hate would be remiss!

With love the common element
Bringing us such peace
That gives us hope for a life
Where love will never cease

The Wind Blows the Trees to Bend

The wind blows the trees to bend
As rivers wend their way
Through fields so ubiquitous
Forever and a day!

I want to run and be the wind
And pause to be the tree
Then wander like a river does
To see what I might be!

And as the day gives way to night
I'll lay me down to rest,
Upon a bed of marigolds
Natures fragrant nest?

I'll dream sweet dreams of harmony
And wake up fresh and new
To start another fruitful day
Not caring what I do!

Then when I reach my journeys end
And make my final rest
I'll know from deep within my heart
I did my very best

Conscience

I know not the proprietor
Nor who the dweller be
I only hear my conscience cry
When I'm too blind to see!

Winters Glow

I look down to see the ground
But all I see instead
Is pure white snow with winters glow,
As if the world were dead?

I look to see the proud green tree
With branches full and strong,
But once again winters been
Singing deaths sad song!

And so I stand in natures land
Confusion in my mind,
As if the beauty and life's duty
have all been left behind!

Then as I walked sweet nature talked
And said be patient man
For in the spring, nearly everything
Will come to life again?

The Mystery of Life

I sit and think of days to come

And what is yet to be

Which will be my future

What will become of me.

No one can tell your fortune

Despite what some may say

The only thing that we can know

Is now and yesterday!

The past is full of memories

Distorted by their age

The present brings to our life's book

Another empty page

The future is uncertain

The mystery of life

To some it brings such sweetness

For others only strife

But we will struggle always

To find that magic key

That will unlock the future

And solve life's mystery?

Love is Like a Gentle Rose

Love is like a gentle rose
You plant the seed watch as it grows
And then it blooms sweet beauties face
To sprout forth gentleness and grace!

A winter comes with pressures plight
And withers beauty from our sight
Replaced with pain and helpless fear
The dew becomes a tiny tear?

The pricking thorn to scratch your heart
To dash your hopes before they start
Then lifeless petals fall to earth
The dye is cast upon your birth!

Oh sweet beauty earthward bound
Dust to dust recycled ground
Springs forth new another bloom
Love is strong within the womb?

Why is what we'd like to know
Like asking why the wind will blow
I have no answer to your pain
Only thoughts that seem insane,

For I am just as blind as you
Confusion racks me thru and thru
For when our seeds of love were sown
We thought we'd never be alone?

And so you see this life's heed
Another rose returns to seed!

Insidious Pains

A feeling of passion
That courses our veins
And tenders the fire's
Of insidious pains!

Is cause for the hermit
To die all alone.
Whether coward or hero
May never be known?

Where is the freedom,
The promise of love.
The gentle persuader
And olive branch dove?

Consider the poet
Betrothed of the mind,
Undaunted trespasser,
So easy to find!

Words are his gadgets,
The pen is his tool.
The spirits cat burglar
Securing the jewel!

Possessor of secrets,
Locked deep within!
A prison of promises
Broken again!

In dimly lit hallways
The echo resounds,
Insanities playground
Of adverbs and nouns!

Oh magical fusion
Of spirit and mind,
We struggle to search,
But never to find!

A feeling of passion
That courses our veins
And tenders the fire
Of insidious pains!

Suicide

I feel the weight of oppression
Slithering through the dampness of my mind?
Mongoose eyes red with night fires
Peering quizzically from the shadows!
Where are the slave ships
The oars
The whips of brutal brandishment?
Our wounds will not heal without air,
And lives of shallow pursuance create,
Then decimate meaning
In the lone chamber of a Russian revolver!

Racers Blood

The smell of burning rubber
Stale gas and heated cars!
These are in a racers blood
And written in his stars!

He tries to find more speed somewhere
In engine and design,
The gas must be a special fuel
So carefully refined!

The feeling is a thrilling one
To sit behind the wheel!
The power of the engine and
The road is what he'll feel!

And when he takes the checkered flag
He knows he's number one
Until the next important race
That he's already won?

Cold and Alone

The disfigured stranger
Who whispers of danger
The dark re-arranger
Of terror unknown

The drifter is scowling
While quietly prowling
The hound dogs are howling
A melodious tone

The night air is chilling
It smells of a killing
And we are not willing
To travel alone

The scene is appalling
As we begin crawling
And people are stalling
Whilst in the zone

The fear and the evil
Like something medieval
Then comes the upheaval
Of times unknown

The feeling of dread
Enters our head
Someday we'll all be dead
Cold and alone

Kicks

I use no illusion
No magic or tricks
A pencil and paper
Give me my kicks?

For I am a poet
A writer of lore
Depicter of passion
And oh so much more?

In hallways of darkness
Alone in my room
In thoughts high angelic
Or up from the tomb?

Time is no master
Yet I am a slave
With one chance for joy
Alone in my grave?

With more than illusions
And magical tricks
With pencil and paper
I get my kicks?

Ode to Ben

I hear a voice

In soft rejoice

Making a solemn vow

Of earth and seas

And pleasantries

That offer only now

So here I stand

In full command

My futures not foreseen

A tabloid of

My spirits love.

For all that might have been!

The Wind Blows the Trees to Bend

The wind blows the trees to bend
As rivers wend there way,
Trough fields so ubiquitous,
Forever and a day!

I want to run and be the wind
And pause to be the tree
Then wander like the river does
To see what I might see?

And as the day gives way to night,
I'll lay me down to rest!
Upon a bed of marigolds
Natures fragrant nest!

I'll dream sweet dreams of harmony
Then wake up fresh and new
To start another wonderful day
Not knowing what I'll do!

Then when I reach my journeys end
And make my final rest?
I'll know from deep within my heart,
I did my very best.

Our Victories Finite!

I've heard it said
In tales of dread
How demons rule the night

Then in the day
They slip away
And disappear from sight

But when the sun
Again is done
When darkness takes control

The terror starts
Within our hearts
And claims our very soul

It's crystal clear
The painful fear
As agony abounds

Suspicion schemes
To haunt our dreams
And make our battle grounds?f

We should retreat
But no defeat
For we will stand and fight!

And claim a win
As we begin
Our victories finite!

Silken Wings

A butterfly will briefly pause
To notice natures simplest cause!
Then goes about it's busy ways
On never ending summer days.
It teases us with beauty brief,
A moments worth of sweet relief
And then it's gone on silken wings
To share its joy with other things!

Cry with the Masses

We are people of different backgrounds
With a singular goal in mind
To achieve a life full of freedom
In a land that's internally blind

So we struggle to keep common sense
To be the rule of the day
And look to our fearless leaders
To show us a better way!

Never mind any rhyme, any reason
Never mind who we grind in the dust
With our careless and plodding footsteps
Defying our very own trust

Listen here people, before you're consumed
By the fires of the hell here below
Where death comes so quickly to others
For you it is painfully slow

Never fret over lost achievements
Always laugh when disaster calls
As for me I will cry with the masses
And lay down with the first one who falls!

Together Forever

If I were a mountain
And you were the sea
I'd find a way
To bring us to be,
Together!

If you were a flower
And I were a tree
I'd find a way
To keep you with me
Forever!

With a heart full of love
And two eyes that can see
With a mind that's wide open
And a conscience that's free!

Then comes the joy of eternity
Together, forever, you and I, we!

To Know the End

The moon is framed by darkened skies,
The amber glow of hidden lies?
The night air sings of alibi's
To hide the fact the sun will rise.

So fear belies, and courage takes
When in this life we make mistakes
For we can't see the writhing snakes
And all the pain the horror makes.

And we don't know if foe or friend
Until we learn how to transcend?
The wind blown branches learn to bend
But we will break to know the end!

Is that We did the Best We Could

We can make an easy climb
If we let the verses rhyme
Go forth now, be lifted up
Drink the wisdom in life's cup!

In this dream of hope and love
As we jostle, push and shove
Our dreams can be a nightmare true
Unless we learn a way to view,

The faith we have in our fellow man,
An attitude of yes we can
Successful people every day
Know how to work and when to play?

And so I bid a fond farewell
Let future generations tell
My one intent as understood
Is that we did the best we could!

Our Final Frontier

Confurion, collusion
My mind is like a whirlpool
Winning, sinning
Like a blinded searching fool?
Continue, sinew
Grasping in the dark
Reaching, preaching
For a thought yet to embark?
Aimlessly, blamelessly
Living life another day
Wondering, blundering
Is there a better way
Employment, enjoyment
Something we search for
Wanting, haunting
Life and so much more
Borrow, sorrow
The churning burning pain
Withering, slithering
Snakes inside the brain
Hoping, groping
Love can break the trance
Showing, knowing
There's only one chance
Praying, playing
Look to God above
Lurching, searching
For the light of love
Reckoning, beckoning
No answer to appear
Lying, dying
And our final frontier!

Balance

I sail on calm, blue seas
With thoughts and feelings
As woven images.
I plot my
Course for least resistance;
And
Sway on liquid furrows of even keel?

Wearing the Present Day Fashion

Love is merely a state of mind,
Enhanced by physical attraction!
Yet when we seek to find that love
It takes a plan of action!

True love is more than the lust you feel
For it's a bewitching sign.
That's haunted man throughout the years
With desire being quite divine.

Another piece of the puzzle is,
The fashion of the day.
Because vanity plays an important role
When love has gone cliché?

So if you want to find true love,
Look for a woman with passion!
She'll do whatever she can while,
Wearing the present day fashion?

A Perfect Stranger Came up to Me

A perfect stranger came up to me
Panting and short of breath.

He wanted to tell me some good news
about his pending death!

His suit was made of hardened steel
And he carried a cumbersome sword!

He spoke to me in a Latin tongue
Telling me he is the Lord!

I laughed so hard I shed a tear;
But had to think again,

For he showed me all the scars
, Where the nails were hammered in!

So I fell upon my knees right there
And offered up a prayer?

I asked him for forgiveness and
To cleanse me, but beware,

For Satan comes in many forms
To trick the weakest link!

As we prepare to meet our God
It's harder than you think,

To live this one and only life
Without a single crime!

So I thought about the stranger then
And his long and painful climb

When suddenly it came to me
For what had happened here?

The foretold story is coming true
and Christ did reappear!

When the Storm Clouds Gathered in

The skies began to darken as the sun was going down,

When I noticed with my one good eye

That clouds began to form!

The wind started picking up as dust began to blow

So I drank it in till I was drunk

And staggered toward the door

When lightning struck a tree out front I think it was an Oak!

I suddenly surrendered to the power and the force

Of mother natures awesomeness?

And helped us to recover

When the storm clouds gathered in!

I Crafted Quite a Work of Art

I crafted quite a work of art
without a painters brush?

Nor did I use a ball of clay
to fabricate a bust

I didn't hammer on a rock
to make a statuette

Or use a piece of charcoal
to draw a silhouette

I used my pen and paper
To write an anecdote

A poem of epic content,
More than a passing note

To bring you back to a realm
Of harsh reality

Where life and death decisions
Come like hyperbole

Art is meant to touch you
in more than just one way

It stirs the love that's in your heart
And causes you to pray

To say it doesn't touch a nerve
and give you pause to think

Is saying to the world in fact,
There is no missing link

Now when you look at art again
Remember this repeat

Enjoy the treasures of the world
Before they're obsolete

Natures Friend

I wrote a poem one wintry night
For all the world to see,
I let them feel the cold crisp air
And touch the barren tree.

I had them walk down icy paths
And see the falling snow,
I brought a crackling fire to them
A warmth of amber glow!

I had them hear the howling wind
Sing mournfully that night,
In chorus with a baying hound
A song of sheer delight.

I painted all my winter scenes
With more than stroke of pen!
You see tis natures very words
Translated by a friend?

Printed in the United States
by Baker & Taylor Publisher Services